Kevin Durant:

The Incredible Story of Kevin Durant - One of Basketball's Greatest Players

Table of Contents

Introduction

Thanks and congratulations for picking up this book, *Kevin Durant: The Incredible Story of Kevin Durant - One of Basketball's Greatest Players.*

The following chapters will discuss the absolutely amazing story of Kevin Durant. Kevin started out a small child in the bustling city of Washington, D.C. and would grow to be one of the most demanded players in the entirety of the game of basketball.

This book details Durant's early life, and the challenges he had to overcome to be the basketball icon we know him as today. You will also learn about his high school and college experiences, as well as his biggest moments in the NBA to date.

You will soon discover what it took for Kevin to become the incredible player he is today, and what might be next for him on his new team.

There is a lot to be learned from Kevin Durant's inspiring story. Thanks once again for choosing this book. I hope you find it to be both informative, as well as motivating! Enjoy!

Chapter 1: Early Life

In 1988, Wanda and Wayne Pratt were expecting a beautiful child. On September 29th of 1988, that child was born. Named Kevin Wayne Durant, the child would spend his early life growing up in Washington D.C.

When Durant was very young, his dad would desert him and his mother, leaving them without the ever important support of a father. However, Durant's grandmother, Barbara Davis, would end up stepping up to the plate and helping to raise him.

As a child, though, Durant's biggest role model would be Taras Brown. When he was young, Durant would spend a very good portion of his time playing basketball and hanging out with peers at the Seat Pleasant Recreation Center. This is where he would meet Mr. Brown. Mr. Brown would ultimately end up coaching Durant's AAU team and becoming, down the line, Durant's godfather.

Growing up, Kevin was always the tallest boy in all of his classes. As a result, he became very self-conscious about his height, sticking out like a sore thumb. Kevin's mother would make accommodations at Kevin's schools, and his grandmother would tell him just to "wait and see."

Kevin, even as a child, was a consistently amazing basketball player. His first noteworthy competition came when he joined the Prince George Jaguars. The Jaguars would win two nation-wide championships while Kevin was on the team. His first national championship happened when he was only 11 years old. In this tournament, he would end up scoring eighteen points in just the 2nd half of the final game. It was after this game, at the age of only eleven, that Kevin knew he wanted to be a basketball player as a career: he was so excited that he told his mom exactly that.

As a part of the Jaguars, he would become best friends with Michael Beasley, as well as Chris Braswell. All three would become professional basketball players later in life.

Kevin's mother and godfather Taras Brown would try to create a program intended to expedite the process of increasing Kevin's already impressive set of basketball skills. The very first rule of this program was that Kevin wasn't allowed to play pickup games - although these games were very enjoyable, they would only serve to reinforce negative habits. In place of pickup games, when Kevin wasn't playing a genuine game, Brown set up a set of drills for Kevin to perform. Kevin would become absolutely addicted to practicing basketball, working on his body and skills for as long as eight hours every day when summer rolled around. Needless to say, Kevin was very appreciative of the set of rules that coach Brown developed and followed them to an absolute tee.

As Kevin became a high school student, he would join the varsity team at Montrose Christian School, located in Rockville Maryland. It was here that his hard work would really start to pay off. Kevin played there as a freshman and sophomore.

The first year for him was rocky. Though he played impressively, his older teammates would be threatened by his immense skill. They would threaten to quit passing the ball to him. Kevin, as a freshman, felt as though he should quit basketball. However, his memories of his mother working herself half to death in order to put food on the table would prompt him to keep going and to do something bigger with basketball. And so, he kept going.

His experience would sweeten as he went into his sophomore year of high school. That year, he would start to become a well-regarded star player. Not only did he gain right about five inches in height, boosting him to a grand total of 6'8", but his second varsity season led him to being named the local Player of the Year afterward. This, surely, was a massive paradigm shift from his first year.

Despite a really strong second season, his third varsity season is where things really started to pick up in a massive way. He transferred to the famous Oak Hill Academy, notorious for pumping out high quality basketball players at a very consistent rate. Here, he would join his old teammate from the Jaguars;

Lawson.

During his junior year Kevin would end up averaging 19.6 points per game and 8.8 rebounds. Parade Magazine would also end up voting him as the *Second Team All-American*. Kevin would spend his junior year at Oak Hill Academy and continue to draft up the beginnings of a major legacy.

His senior year of varsity was the altogether biggest pre-professional year for him. The years of hard work constituting of constantly drilling himself, practicing every spare moment that he had, and playing a seemingly endless number of organized games would finally culminate into something bigger for him. It was at this point that the nucleus of his dream - becoming a professional basketball player - had reached its final form.

In his senior year, Durant would end up becoming a player for the endlessly famous National Christian Academy. It was here that he would come under the guidance of Stu Vetter, an incredible legend of a coach. Here, he would manage still to improve himself. So much so, in fact, that his averages would rise from 19.6 points per game to 23.6 points per game. His rebounds, too, would shoot up: from 8.8 rebounds per game to 10.9.

His impressive performance put him on the map in quite a lot of ways. For example, McDonald's named Durant an All-American and he then played at their 2006 All-Star Game. It was at the McDonald's All-Star Game that he would be named one of the MVPs. This was just one small thing which showed the immense success of Durant. The point is that he was being eyed by pretty much every single major college basketball program in America.

This was in part because of his incredible ability, but there was another element to it. Even going back to his early years of basketball, Durant had an amazing game sense and would try to get his teammates to follow his lead. Even going back to his junior high basketball days, his team often wouldn't make a real and finite "play" in any sense but would rather just let Kevin control the speed of the game and the flow of it, too. It was this ability to not only lead, but to corral his teammates behind his leadership that partially put Durant on the map.

Another part of it, too, was that even at his impressive final height - 6'9" - he still retained both a high level of speed, and impeccable instincts for the game. Almost nobody in all of the varsity league was able to lay a finger on Kevin or keep him from making shots. He was so skilled, too, that if he needed or wanted to snag points, it seemed that he could almost automatically do so just by sheer force of will. And after his intense practice regimens and countless hours dedicated to the sport, that was almost the situation: an impossibly good skill for knowing what needed to be done at any point and when, supplemented by thousands of hours of practice making it completely feasible regardless of what it was.

Needless to say, there were a lot of people wanting Kevin at this point. He was the apple of college basketball team's eye in a lot of ways, and represented what pretty much every team wants: raw, fresh, young talent; somebody who's willing to go above and beyond, and be what can only be described as an absolute torrent on the field or the court.

One of the most notable instances of Durant's courtship by various colleges was when the previously mentioned Ty Lawson would tirelessly try to get Kevin to accompany him to the University of North Carolina at Chapel Hill to play for the Tar Heels. Being an alum of the University of North Carolina at Chapel Hill is an honor in and of itself, but their basketball program is absolutely legendary. The Tar Heels men's basketball team has gone on to generate a ton of massively notable professional basketball players. What's more is that they made three of the greatest basketball players in history, the most recognizable of whom is the endlessly famous Michael Jordan.

Alas, it wasn't the Tar Heels that would end up catching Kevin Durant's fancy. It was indeed the University of Texas that would eventually get Kevin to sign. This was in large part due to Russell Springmann. Springmann at the time was as an assistant at the University. However, he'd for a long time maintained contact with Durant, seeing his potential from the very beginning. In fact, he'd been in touch with Kevin since his very first year of varsity basketball. The other primary factor was Maurice Evans, who played at that point for the Lakers. Evans was an alum of the University of Texas. He would end up training with Durant a fair amount and would play a heavy part in the courting of Durant to come to the University.

There's quite a bit to be said about Kevin's early life, and in fact, it could be a book in and of itself. It was largely what shaped him into the man he is today. Indeed, some factors are underplayed or underappreciated. For example, Kevin's father abandoned him early, this is true. However, in Kevin's adolescence, his father would actually come back and then take him to various basketball games and tournaments all over the country.

It's rough and, indeed, almost impossible to reduce something so multifaceted as somebody's childhood into simple little axioms that can pertly define somebody's end result, and it's even harder (if it's possible) to attempt to draw accurate lines between somebody's childhood or other parts to their *present*. Certainly, you can tuck things away into little boxes and try to organize them cutely, but doing so is in and of itself a challenge.

To do so with Kevin's childhood and adolescence is likewise difficult. There are so many factors which come to play in somebody's life that it's almost impossible to pick one or two out of a hat. This is equally true for Kevin.

For whether we're talking about his father's absence and the same man's eventual return, his mother's working multiple jobs just to put food on the table and to try to make sure Kevin could make his own dreams come true, his grandmother for filling in the spaces and voids that Kevin's father left, or the man who would come to be known as Kevin's godfather for drilling him endlessly and helping him to make something of himself by giving him a finite plan and infinite moral support, it's rather difficult to peg down what made Kevin who he is in an exact man.

One thing is clear, however: all of it taught Kevin some very vital lessons - on impermanence, on perseverance, on endless effort, on putting in one hundred and ten percent even when it's for a dream that seems unreachable or downright impossible. It is all of these lessons, in conjunction with the people who would raise him and mold him, that would make

Kevin Durant the person that he is.

But a childhood is only a foundation. That foundation is something that he would have to build upon going forward.

In building upon it, he would become one of the most celebrated modern professional basketball players and end up as what can truly only be accurately described as a force to be reckoned with. The foundation gave him the stability to endure whatever stormy days came his way, and were vital in him pushing him further, even for his single year in college.

That is exactly what we'll be discussing next: his year in college. However, when talking about Kevin Durant, the college years can be considered as formative as anything else; formative, wholly, to creating a living legend.

Chapter 2: College Career

When Kevin started at the University of Texas, they were under the coaching tutelage of a man named Rick Barnes. Rick Barnes is a phenomenal man of his own accord.

The Longhorns before Barnes were iffy. As with any team, they had their ups and downs due to various reasons. Shifting rosters, coaching shifts, and simply bad luck had set them on a course best described as average. Barnes, however, changed that. Any sports fan knows that a team's coach is every bit as important as their star player. A bad coach makes a bad team, and a good coach makes a good team better. Fortunately for the Longhorns, Barnes was a good coach. The beginning of Barnes' coaching tenure signaled a hopeful end of the Texas Longhorn's monsoon season and a phenomenal return to form. He produced several seasons with upwards of twenty wins and had a huge number of appearances at NCAA tournaments - often enough that you can reliably say that it was in large part due to Barnes' expert coaching and not just some fluke.

It was certainly enticing to Kevin to join one of the most phenomenal teams in the history of college basketball. What's more is that various courtiers were looming promises of Kevin starting on the team - even as a college freshman, which is incredibly impressive - and finishing the season with the world's eyes on him due to his immense skill. Nobody could turn that down. Durant, smartly, joined on.

It was a combination of the University of Texas Tar Heels' impeccable roster - bolstered, no less, by Kevin Durant - and the incredible coaching ability of Rick Barnes that made it seem like the University basketball team had an amazing shot at breaking some records during Kevin's freshman year.

Barnes held a certain respect for Durant. Initially, Barnes intended to simply draft plays for the team, as always. Such is the standard mode for a coach of a basketball team, right? Corral their individual talents into one cohesive unit, which you then put everything that you can into driving towards victory.

This, however, was not the case during Durant's tenure on the Longhorns. Barnes held so much respect for Durant's absurdly good game sense that he simply let Kevin call the shots for the most part.

It was a solid plan. Barnes realized that doing anything else would be an affront to the freshman Durant's immense talent for not only feeling how the game *was* going, but also knowing where it *should be going*.

Letting Kevin take the reins was a solid plan. For as long as Kevin's teammates were on board with simply letting Kevin dictate how the game would go, what would result would usually be a win. Despite being in the incredibly intimidating NCAA, Kevin still maintained as firm of a grip as always, and in fact managed to get an even stronger one. The rougher competition naturally made Kevin improve at a consistent rate comparable to the difficult new set of competitors which now faced him.

Despite this set of challenges, Kevin stayed extraordinarily headstrong and would be an important part in leading the team to victory. Between Durant, teammate A.J. Abrams, and Coach Barnes, the Longhorns were shared between three sets of incredibly capable hands.

Everything would indeed pay off by the end of the season; Durant's teammates naturally felt an initial reluctance to fully invest their trust in the hotshot freshman starter but, by the end of the season, the Longhorns would have a stunning twenty-five victories, and only ten losses.

What did this mean for the Longhorns? It means that they were in third place of the Big 12 conference, as well as in the top twenty NCAA basketball teams nationwide.

Abrams and Kevin would maintain their de facto leadership spots and fight tooth and nail in order to claw their way to the Big 12 conference's championship game. In this game, the Longhorns were up against the Kansas Jayhawks, fighting for the conference championship title. The game was an absolute hailstorm, and would become one of the biggest comebacks for the Jayhawks in history.

At one point, the Longhorns were beating the Jayhawks immensely. They managed to spring a massive comeback. During the second half of the game, Craig Winder from the Longhorns fatally missed a throw, a move which allowed the Jayhawks to get a three-pointer which would tie the game. The game then went into overtime. In the very last seconds of the game, Durant had a chance to score for the win with a layup.

And he missed it.

Regardless of this, Durant still led the scoreboards, with an amazing 37 points scored individually.

Anyhow, despite a massive letdown for the Longhorns, Durant and the team charged on. They still finished in second place and they ended up getting fourth seed in the East Regional NCAA Tournament. This is where things would end up getting iffy.

The first game was easy, all things considered. The Longhorns won out against the New Mexico State Aggies with a score of 79 to 67. There is little phenomenal about this game in any terms.

Soaring with championship dreams and elation after a well-earned first win, the team headed into the second game. In this game, the Longhorns would face off against the University of South Carolina Gamecocks. After a hardfought game, they would end up succumbing to the Gamecocks, losing 87 to 68.

This was a crushing defeat for the Longhorns. However, they still reveled in the fact that they made it amazingly far. And what signified a defeat for the Longhorns only represented another beginning for Durant.

Durant would decide that his college basketball career was, hopefully, over; not out of anger or desperation, no, but out of the desire to go onto something bigger.

Indeed, he would only be in the college basketball circuit for one year, but he would learn quite a bit during this year. He would savor both victory and defeat when neither seemed to come as expected. More than that, he would - for arguably the first time - play against "serious" opponents that gave him a genuine challenge. Durant would learn that college basketball was a whole different "ballgame" than the varsity teams that he was used to.

With the end of his college career surfacing, Kevin was boasting some amazing end-of-year statistics. Throughout his season, he would have averaged about twenty-six points per game, alongside a whole eleven rebounds per game. He also would end up having twenty games wherein he scored thirty or more points, which is incredibly impressive. He also had the third-most boards by a freshman in the entire history of the NCAA, coming in with a grand total of 390.

Indeed, his impressive college year signified something bigger yet to come: an absolutely incredible pro career, which cemented the legend around Durant and made him a figure to aspire to.

Chapter 3: Making the NBA

Shortly after the disappointing loss to the Gamecocks in the second game of the NCAA Division I invitational, Kevin would give up his remaining college eligibility, and declare his own eligibility for the yearly NBA draft.

He and Greg Oden were two of the most hotly contested people to declare for the draft in the 2008 preseason. Indeed, there were few people that could even come near matching up to the two. Both would end up being the contested first pick of the season after extremely impressive showings in the NCAA the season prior.

Oden would end up being the first to be picked, being picked up by the Portland Trailblazers. Kevin would be the second pick, being picked up by the Seattle Supersonics.

Pretty soon after being drafted, Durant also landed his first major endorsement. Actually, this was one of the bigger endorsements ever cut in professional basketball, and it was especially high at the time. The deal that would end up being cut was between him and Nike for a $60-million-dollar endorsement contract. The terms were that he would wear and endorse Nike products for seven years, at which point the contract would run out. This was only overshadowed at the time by LeBron James' contract - also with Nike - that was a fair bit more. It seemed that even the major corporations at the time knew that they were dealing with what could hardly be described better than by the word "phenom".

During his rookie season, Durant made a lot of strides personally. It's no surprise; his incredibly offensive play style made him an absolute terror on the court. Nobody could keep up with him due to his stature, speed, and skill. And what's more is that while he was menacing to his enemies, he was proving to be a great asset to his teammates. His ability to reliably shoot and score from almost anywhere on the court made him a massive boon for scoring opportunities throughout any given game, it seemed.

Where Kevin fell short in his first season was his defensive play. He found it difficult to defend against others, both bigger and smaller. Bigger opponents were simply stronger, and would be able to massively overpower him. Meanwhile, smaller opponents were able to outmaneuver him and essentially go right past him. However, his game sense would prove to be a viable replacement where he lacked physically, and his dedication would also make him insanely driven to improve his defensive play. Over time, he would find himself becoming a much better defensive player, using his advantages - his sense for the game, his handiness with the ball, his seemingly innate ability for understanding the flow of the game - as a way to fill in the blanks where needed.

The Seattle Supersonics had two rookies on board. There was, of course, Durant, but there was also Jeff Green. With Durant and Green as a dynamic forward duo, the Supersonics would have one of the strongest offensive lines in the entirety of pro basketball at the time. Indeed, the two would be named NBA Rookie First Teamers, and rightfully so - they both were incredibly bright players with an insane amount of game knowledge and a very strong intuition.

The season didn't start off beautifully for Kevin, with many of his first professional games being losses. However, even in these losses, he still managed to shine incredibly brightly as an individual player, scoring - for example - eighteen points against the Denver Nuggets. It was also rather early in the season that Kevin Durant would, for the first time in his pro career, land the game-winning shot. In a tense game against the Atlanta Hawks, things had long been tied. The game had finally gone into double overtime. Kevin would end up scoring the three-point shot which pushed the game over the edge and secured the win for the Seattle Supersonics.

Regardless of Durant's generally nearly flawless play, the Supersonics wouldn't perform terribly well in Durant's first season. Indeed, in the '07-'08 season, they would only manage to secure about twenty wins altogether - a tad disappointing. Despite the losses, Durant still managed - in his typical fashion - to garner the spotlight and steer the focus towards his expert play and incredible sense of the game.

At the end of the season, there were major changes in store for the Seattle Supersonics. After he was unable to get a new arena built in Seattle, the team owner Clay Bennett opted to move the team back to his childhood home, Oklahoma City. It took a bit of time to square away all of the legal details, but it was eventually worked out in time before the '08-'09 season could begin. The team was promptly renamed to the 'Oklahoma City Thunder', which remains their name to this day.

The team's premiere season as the Oklahoma City Thunder would be marginally better. Alongside the thunderous duo of Durant and Green would join another amazing player - Russell Westbrook. Westbrook, Durant, and Green would form a basis for an absolutely incredible line-up which would be a force to be reckoned with once everybody started to gel. Beyond the three were several other players who did a great job filling out the team's line-up.

The team's inaugural season started off in what is, quite honestly, a terrible manner. The team's coach at the time, P.J. Carlesimo, ended up proving incredibly ineffectual. He didn't prove to be a very effective coach in terms of bringing three absolutely incredible talents together.

After having only one victory to buffer out twelve defeats, Carlesimo was fired. He was replaced by the interim coach Scott Brooks, who would coach the rest of the season. The team's record would not make much of a comeback. In fact, the ratio would stay about the same. By the end of the season, they'd have a .280 win/loss ratio, nabbing up 23 wins and 59 losses.

However, in the face of all of these demoralizing losses, the team didn't lose steam. In fact, they would only grow closer together and start to play even more cohesively. By the end of the season, they would win by 41 points over the Los Angeles Clippers, pulling an exciting almost cliffhanger-esque end to their season which left all hopeful Thunder fans saying: "What now?"

Scott Brooks, after the Clippers win, was promoted from the interim coach of the Thunder to the full-time coach, which proved an exciting promise of more to come.

During the inaugural season of the Oklahoma City Thunder, Kevin still managed to improve his performance. He, at this point, was starting to adjust even better to the pressures of professional basketball and the more difficult competition. His average points per game went up to twenty-five, and he hit a little under half of all of his shots. He also bumped his rebound game up, getting nearly seven rebounds every single night.

The new coaching prowess found in Brooks, alongside the almost storybook ending of the season prior, meant that there was a lot of mystique surrounding the Oklahoma City Thunder's second season. People were looking forward to seeing in full force what the previous season had hinted at: the beautiful result of the necessary lubrication to turn the Thunder into a well-oiled machine. Whether it was the coaching staff, internal conflict, a sort of "tilting" (where you start to lose solely because losses put you in a negative state of mind), luck, or any combination thereof, what was most important was that the Thunder were headed in a positive direction. And more than that, they were headed in a direction which would finally mean that people could see the amazing talents of Westbrook, Durant, and Green playing off of one another.

Experts, at the beginning of the second season of the Thunder, began to recognize the immense talent of the team's members, and expected that they would be able to make some very important accomplishments. Coach Brooks took these expectations to heart, and he started drilling the idea of meeting those expectations into his players. The second season wouldn't signify any major trades; the core of Westbrook, Durant, and Green would remain. The only players which would be traded were the more expendable ones. Likewise, no major players would leave.

The very beginning of the season painted the Thunder out to be what they wanted to be the two seasons before: a *team*. They weren't making any amazing accomplishments, but they were doing what they'd failed to do in a great capacity before: working with one another, instead of somehow managing to work against one another. No longer did the gears of the Thunder grind against one another, but rather they worked off of one another in unison, making the machine finally work as it was supposed to. While the earlier part of the season wasn't terribly impressive, it represented what wasn't there before: a very strong foundation that the team could build upon. For once, it seemed as though the team had nowhere to go but *up*.

Sure enough, that's exactly what would happen. The second half of the Thunder's second season and Durant's third professional season would be where they absolutely kicked it into overdrive. The decision of Coach Brooks and team owner Clay Bennett to only trade off the expendable parts and build a base off of Westbrook, Durant, and Green would turn out to be an absolutely amazing and incredibly smart decision. The Thunder would end up getting a nine-game streak that would propel them to, for the first time as the Thunder, hit fifty season wins. They did exactly that. Along the way, they would qualify for the playoffs, another milestone as the Thunder. Though they would lose out in the first round of the Western conference, making the playoffs was still a tremendous honor one way or another. Plus, let's be honest - going 2-4 against the immensely impressive Lakers isn't exactly something to sneeze at.

Indeed, perhaps the most impressive part of the whole affair was the manner in which they held up against some of the league's strongest teams. Even against such legendary teams as the Orlando Magic, the Los Angeles Lakers, and the Boston Celtics, they would manage to pull out blowout wins and pull off massive upsets.

As usual, the star of the show was Durant. Durant, at this point, was solidifying his legend status, and had given an amazing amount of leverage to the Thunder in almost all of their games during the season. The Thunder's second season was the one where Durant would truly become the king of the hill in

16

terms of the NBA's best leaders, and despite his relative lack of experience, he never faltered from hitting shots every time it counted.

Perhaps more important was the fact that he served as a bit of an emotional rock during the entire process. When things would go south - as they will even with the most solid of teams - Durant was there, providing wisdom, confidence, and finesse. It would spread like wildfire and serve as a springboard for his team to simply keep their cool and, more often than not, make a comeback.

As mentioned previously, Kevin firmly cemented his legend status in the Thunder's second season, and it wasn't by simply by the word of it; Durant would set several records over the course of the season. For example, he broke the NBA record for number of games in a row where a player scored at least 25 points, with a staggering 29 games in a row. Durant also broke the record of most consecutive thirty-point games, which had stood for nearly forty years as conquered by basketball legend Spencer Haywood, when Durant smashed the record by having seven thirty-plus games in a row. He also managed to have several forty-point games.

The end of the season saw Kevin average a staggering 30.1 points per game. This is amazing in and of itself. He managed to just barely outscore basketball legend LeBron James in order to become the scoring champion of the NBA that year. What's more is that with him being so young - only 21 and a half years old at the time - Kevin would become known as the youngest scoring champ in the entirety of the NBA's long history.

Immediately after game 6 of the Thunder's first-round playoff run, where they would lose the series to the Lakers, Durant got to work on getting his team on track for the next season. As the old saying goes, there's no rest for the wicked; indeed, it seemed there was no rest for the young and ambitious Durant either. In the locker room, he told his teammates that the following season started right that moment. He told them that they had no option but to start thinking like champions and, indeed, working as hard as champions would work, right then and there. His tone, though, wasn't angry - nor was it vindictive, melancholy, or crushed. Rather, it was hopeful. He was, as always, acting as the rock for his team in their times of crisis. He told them that every team that will be the ultimate victor must suffer through horrible losses.

Regardless of the crushing end to the Thunder's second season, this marked the beginning of an upturn in Kevin's career. No longer was his team getting a .275 win ratio. No longer was his team failing to mesh. The truth is that the season had been an incredible one, and if everything before was a down, then the Thunder's second season marked the beginning of a very big up.

The up would begin to show itself, too. At the end of the season, just before the start of the preseason, Kevin nearly clinched the franchise's prestigious MVP honor. Durant, of course, was no stranger to being crowned MVP. Regardless, he would end up placing second, losing out to the legendary LeBron James.

That summer, Durant, James, and several other star players were chosen to be on the All-NBA First Team. He also would have a summer full of promotions and endorsement drudgery to work through. What fans of the Thunder were looking forward to, understandably, was the coming season.

It would actually be a very bright and strong season. The Thunder had their eyes on the prize again. Where their season as the Seattle Supersonic and their inaugural season as the Thunder was spent simply trying to mesh and work together, and their second season as the Thunder was spent simply trying to perform better than they had before, their strong showing in the second season meant that Durant knew he and his team could end up taking over the league and being crowned champions.

The season started off without any major roster changes. It also started off with a very convincing win against the Chicago Bulls, a timeless team who at the time also had a lot of young players with boundless potential. This set the tone for an absolutely excellent season.

A slight roadblock came in the middle of the season when the longtime standard in the Thunder trifecta, Green, was traded out for Kendrick Perkins. The initial shift in team chemistry was hardly noticeable, and the team continued charging through the season without a hitch. Perkins also made up for a lot of where Green fell short, and provided a presence on the court which the Thunder seemed to be missing. Despite the inevitable chemistry hiccups behind closed doors, the team never faltered, and ended up netting an insanely impressive fifty-five wins over the course of the season. They ended as the undoubted Northwest Division champions. Over the course of the season, Durant managed to maintain his spot as scoring champion, and even improved - where he previously had just beat out LeBron James, he now was a full point ahead of him, averaging an incredible 27.7 points per game.

The postseason, as always, was where the biggest challenges would come. The Thunder, however, were firmly intent on coming away as the ultimate champions of the NBA post-season.

Their first round of games was against the Denver Nuggets. This series, at first, seemed like a cinch. The Thunder would take three of the first four games that they played against the Nuggets. Despite this, Denver wouldn't relent. They showed a lot of fight in game five and seemed to be winning, but Durant pulled off an insane comeback by scoring sixteen points in the last twelve minutes of the game. He would end up nabbing a total of forty-one points over the whole game, which was extremely impressive. The fourth win for the Thunder meant that they were moving onto the next series in the conference bracket.

The following series would place them up against the Memphis Grizzlies. Nobody really expected the Grizzlies to do as well as they did during the playoffs, and certainly not the Thunder. The Thunder would lose two of the initial three games. If they lost two more games, they would be in the same position they were in the year prior - they knew they had to fight back.

It was in game four that the Thunder started to fire on all cylinders, doing whatever they could to bring the series back into their favor. They managed to just narrowly do it after an incredibly intense double-overtime game and clinched the victory in the name of the Thunder.

Game five carried on with no major bumps in the road, nor any real Cinderella stories worth noting. However, due to their first losses, they were now 3-2 and would have to win one more game to end the series and move onto the conference finals. They simply weren't able to win game six. The Grizzlies had the home court advantage, and for whatever reason, Durant just couldn't make most of his shots.

At this point, it was now three to three in the Grizzlies-Thunder series, and nobody knew how game seven would go. While the Thunder were obvious favorites going into the series, the Grizzlies had massively shown up and turned everyone's expectations upside down. Nobody knew what would come next. However, the Thunder wanted the NBA crown, and had a ton of pressure on them going into game seven.

You know that old cliché that it takes pressure to make a diamond? Well, the pressure going into game seven turned into a diamond for the Thunder. Perhaps in an attempt to make up for his terrible performance in game six, Kevin would manage to drop 39 points for the team. The Thunder would end up winning by fifteen points in game seven, with a score of 105 to 90. The Thunder were ecstatic with their win in one of the most beautifully intense series of the year. They would go on, as they hoped, to the conference finals.

The conference finals saw the Thunder facing off against the Dallas Mavericks. Sadly, the Thunder would only pull out one win in this series. Game 2 saw the Thunder pull off a miraculous on-the-road win against the Mavericks. However, Dallas would end up victorious in every other game of the series, pushing the Thunder out of contention for the title.

They, understandably, were upset. They didn't get the crown that they were hoping for. However, this wouldn't stop them from pushing forward and trying with all their might to win the championship the following season.

It was perhaps the 2011/2012 season, the Thunder's third season, that would prove to be one of the highlights of Durant's career. It seemed as though everything had built up to this season for Durant. Every last defeat, every long night drilling, every day going from 6am to dinner with his personal trainer, all of it seemed to culminate in his fourth NBA season. It was undoubtedly the most impressive showing of the Thunder to date.

The season would see the Thunder build on everything they'd built up heretofore. The core of the team, built on Durant, Westbrook, and Perkins, were now gelling perfectly. The season got off to a bit of a late start due to the labor negotiations between the basketball players and their team's owners. As such, less games were played overall. Regardless, the Thunder still walked away with an absolutely baffling .712 win ratio, with a record of 47 wins to 19 losses.

This season would also see James Harden and Serge Ibaka add quite a bit to the team's starting lineup, as well. For once, the team wasn't just one or two people leading at a time, but rather a finely tuned cohesive basketball machine, working off of one another in an almost perfect way. Every single member had something to contribute, and it all culminated in making one of the fiercest teams in the NBA at the time.

The primary season went as one would expect: Durant did a number for his team, as per usual. He was an absolute monster on the court and a rock off the court. The post-season is where the team would really start to shine, however.

For so long, the team had been focused on the notion of a championship; of walking away from the NBA as the supreme champions, winning the crown and the glory. They were just as intent this season.

The first series of the playoffs was against the Dallas Mavericks. There were any number of factors which may have contributed. Perhaps it was partly due to the team's mutual desire to see the Mavericks crash and burn after Dallas ruined the Thunder's bid for the finals the year prior. Maybe it was the fact that every single element of the team was into the game. Maybe the conditions were perfect, maybe the weather was right, there are so many "maybes" - but the concrete end result was amazing.

Through two home games and two away games, the Thunder absolutely launched a full assault against the Mavericks. They crushed them with a 4-0 sweep. Perhaps more impressive is that three of the games were extremely close.

Game 1 of the series saw the Thunder win by a *single* point. The only game which wasn't as close was the third game of the series, wherein the Thunder won by 16 points. Every other game was within a margin of six points.

Regardless of the reason and regardless of the point proximity, the key takeaway is that the Thunder won, and that win signified their moving on to the next contender: the Lakers. The Lakers put up a strong fight against the Thunder, but still couldn't edge them out.

The first game saw the Thunder beat the Lakers by nearly an amazing thirty points. This gave the team the momentum that they needed in order to continue winning. Durant would carry game two, getting the game's highest points, highest rebounds, and highest assists. The Thunder would win game two by only two points.

Game three of this series signified the first major hang-up in the Thunder's series run. The Lakers exacted revenge and would edge the Thunder out by three points, ending their six game playoff win streak. Despite their loss, Durant still scored over thirty points for the game.

The Thunder, however, were most certainly in no mood to be kicked out of the conference before the finals and somehow make less progress than they had the year before. They would end up winning games four and five, moving them onto the conference finals.

The performance of the Thunder in the 2012 playoff conference finals is one of their most impressive performances to date. Throughout the entire six game series, Durant was in overdrive, leading the team in points every single game.

The conference finals would pit the Oklahoma City Thunder against the San Antonio Spurs. This series would at times be both devastating and amazing to Oklahoma City fans.

The first two games went to the Spurs. There were a lot of disadvantages. Despite the fact that Durant was on point throughout the entire series, the Spurs just simply edged them out. It certainly didn't help that the two games were on San Antonio's turf, putting Oklahoma's players out of their element.

However, in the third game, the Thunder decided they'd had enough, and that they weren't about to be kicked out of another conference final. The team kicked into overdrive and would pull out a twenty-point win over the Spurs in front of a crowd of nearly 18,000 people at the Chesapeake Energy Arena. This win would lead to another in game four, which would lead to another, and then another. The Thunder ended up miraculously reverse sweeping the Spurs out of the tournament, leading to them making it to the NBA Finals for the first - and the last - time.

The Thunder were absolutely elated. Finally, after years of constant progress and small steps forward, they were within reach of the crown that every single player on the team had dreamt of since childhood.

The NBA finals for the 2012 season would pit the Oklahoma City Thunder against the Miami Heat.

The Thunder, coasting on elation and pure vigor for the win, would win game 1 by 11 points on their home turf. Durant would contribute an amazing 36 points this game.

All factors set the Thunder up for an amazing trajectory. Durant for the last several years had been gradually building up for this moment. Year after year after year, he had drilled endlessly, played on countless middle school and varsity teams, spent a year on the college basketball circuit, lasted through two terrible seasons as a professional player where he hard carried his team to victory, acted as a rock and rallying point for his team his entire professional career, spent long days training, and forced himself to adjust high pressure basketball games against rough opponents, constantly against a curve that seemed to be getting ever tougher, all in order to obtain that moment. That moment where the cheering crowd at the Chesapeake Energy Arena invigorated him and guided him to scoring 36 points against one of the strongest teams in NBA history, where the pressure seemed to melt away, where he was totally in the game, and where - at last - the NBA championship title that he'd dreamt of since his childhood, shooting hoops and training on the plan that his godfather developed while his mother worked endlessly just to put food on the table to make sure Kevin could pursue his dreams, was within an arm's reach.

It was so close that Durant felt he could just reach out and grab it, and he tried, and every time he tried, he would shoot, and those shots would lead to him carrying his team in game 1 of the 2012 NBA Finals. It was, quite literally, a dream come true for Durant. He was what his team rested on. He was the great player he'd always dreamt of becoming. He had become a legend, like he always wanted. The last thing for him to do was to simply grab the title and he could be satisfied, cemented in NBA history as a champion and not as a footnote. The first game meant he had the trajectory. He knew exactly how close he was. But alas, it was not to be.

The Oklahoma City Thunder would lose game two, 96-100.

The Oklahoma City Thunder would lose game three, 85-91.

The Oklahoma City Thunder would lose game four, 98-104.

The Oklahoma City Thunder would lose game five, 106-121.

With a clean sweep, the Miami Heat stole the series and caused Durant's dreams of being the champion to disappear into vapor. It was a crushing defeat for Durant and the Thunder. Despite Durant putting out his best work throughout the series, scoring the highest points for his team in every game except game four where Russell Westbrook dropped an awe-inspiring 43 points, he simply couldn't make it happen.

After the Thunder's third season, they wouldn't get as close to the championship as they had that time. Harden, who'd been an excellent player that year, would go to the Houston Rockets the following season. Though they would improve on their season performance in the following seasons and come out on top in both their divisions and conference in the 2012-2013 season, injuries to Westbrook would cause them to fail to rise to the occasion as they'd had the tendency to do before.

The 2013-2014 season would see their record slightly decline. They'd place 1st in their division once again, but would be eliminated in their conference finals.

The 2014-2015 season was devastating for the Thunder. Injuries would massively result in their loss of steam. Durant underwent surgeries for various issues and wouldn't be able to play. Brooks' coaching went downhill alongside Durant's absence, and the Thunder would fail to make playoffs for the first time since he'd started coaching. He was fired after the season's end.

The 2015-2016 season would mark Durant's last season with the Thunder. Scott was replaced by Billy Donovan. The team would make it to playoffs but would be eliminated once more in the conference finals, marking the third time that they were eliminated in the conference finals and the fourth time making it to the conference finals overall.

Durant's contract with the Thunder came to an end at the conclusion of the 2015-2016 season and he would move on to the Golden State Warriors. As of the time of this writing, the Golden State Warriors are a powerhouse. They've been called a super-team, and for good reason: Durant isn't the only star player on the team. Durant is backed up by Stephen Curry, Klay Thompson, and Draymond Green. What this means is that the team has four all-star players on the starting roster.

During the 2016-17 regular season, they managed to secure an incredible .813 win ratio - higher than Durant had ever experienced on the Thunder.

So what do we know about Kevin's story? It's a rollercoaster. A constant flow up and down. His tenure on the Thunder peaked during the team's third season and the team failed to reach the same position in the seasons following due to a combination of player injuries and failures on behalf of the coaching staff. However, Durant is still incredibly young. He's only 28. That's four years younger than LeBron James, who Durant seems to always be compared to anyhow.

Maybe this means that his best days are ahead of him, and he'll finally be able to take home that championship he's been dreaming of since his youth. Regardless of what happens, what we know for sure is that the Thunder may have peaked, but Durant almost certainly hasn't. He has a while ahead of him to make his mark on basketball history even more than he already has. And if we can take Durant's past determination as any indication, then we can be certain that if he has the opportunity to do something great, he will. Being the world's greatest is no exception. He's already most of the way there.

Conclusion

Thank for making it through to the end of *Kevin Durant: The Incredible Story of Kevin Durant - One of Basketball's Greatest Players*, let's hope it was informative and inspiring for you.

The next step is to analyze Kevin's story and his personality. There's a lot to be learned here. In fact, there's almost an endless amount of things to learn.

If there's one thing that we can take away from Durant's amazing story, though, it's perseverance. Every legend has a lesson to teach. Some teach patience. Some teach the power of knowledge. Durant teaches perseverance and determination.

Think about it this way: Durant's journey has never been easy. The odds were always stacked against him. As a child, he grew up fatherless, operating off of nothing but a love for the game and raw talent. He had the fortune to have good influences in his mother and godfather figure, who were willing to put nearly everything they had into making sure he became all that he wanted to be. However, it never got easier. In high school, he wanted to quit, remember? But he didn't. He stuck it out.

Going through college, he had to face off against tougher opponents and drudge through college basketball for a year before he would be allowed to play professionally. And his professional career is dotted with moments which would prove frustrating. However, instead of just quitting, retiring, or trading off, Durant put his head in the game and remained calm and collected regardless of the circumstances. He made it through terrible seasons, a crushing defeat in the finals, and continues to play to this day on what is arguably the best team that he's ever been on.

Maybe we can apply this same ideal to our daily lives. How often do we get frustrated with things and simply give up? How many times do we wimp out of something because it's something that we see as "too hard" or "not worth the time"? Durant didn't quit when his teammates made his life horrible during his freshman year of high school, nor did he quit when the championship he'd dreamt of his whole life was ripped away from him in a four-game sweep by the Heat.

Durant, plain and simply, doesn't give up. It's amicable, and it's something that we can all learn from.

The legends are lessons for a reason. Part of it is raw talent - probably 90% of it is raw talent, actually. But there's a well-known cliché that determined practice beats undetermined talent almost always. Even if we're naturally talented at something, it doesn't matter if we don't have the determination to make something happen with it.

Durant has the same quality that every other legend has, regardless of their craft. Durant is a sports virtuoso in the same way that Van Gogh was an art virtuoso and Mozart was a piano virtuoso. All of them displayed a natural talent for what they were doing at a young age, but that talent wouldn't have meant anything at all if they wouldn't have taken the time to develop the talent into a demonstrable and worthwhile skill.

So next time that things get hard and you find yourself wanting to quit, you need to think to yourself - "What would Kevin Durant do?" I can almost guarantee you that you can't think of a time where the answer would be "quit" or "give up", because if his enthralling and incredible life story has taught us anything, it's that he doesn't know the meaning of those words.

If you want to be a legend, you must act like a legend, and that starts by learning from legends. And when it comes to building your character, your determination, and yourself in general, Kevin Durant is certainly not a bad model to have.

Finally, if you found this book useful in anyway, a review on Amazon is always appreciated!

Printed in Great Britain
by Amazon